LOVE

BY

J.Grandison

1st Edition Published:

Published by J. Grandison

Cover Design by: Wilde Design

Cover Model: NA

Photographer: NA

Editing by: KA Matthews

Formatting by:

This book is dedicated to my uncle Dale who died at the age of nineteen due to childhood Leukemia.

Table of Contents

Chapter1.

What is it about the winter season that's so invigorating? The snow, the cold temperature? For me, it's all of that. I love winter.

Looking out the big front window of the crappy, little greasy spoon, called Country Kitchen, that I work at as a short order cook, I take in my surroundings of the town I love. The diner is closed, and clean up was easy tonight since there is extra staff on due to the holiday season. I'm just waiting on the busboy, Joe, to finish the dishes so we can go home. I watch some kids slide on the ice that has formed in the street and the people walking by as they window shop. The snow is shimmering like a sea of diamonds under the street lights as more flakes slowly fall to earth. The little town I live in, Glorieville, Ohio, only has about 2,000 residents. So, everybody knows everybody.

I left here once upon a time...

Cindy Grove didn't want to be a small-town housewife, knitting, baking pies, attending hometown sports events. No, she wanted the bright lights of the big city, so we moved to New York, Manhattan to be exact. The Grove family was well-off and well-known. Richard Grove, Cindy's dad, was a very successful real-estate developer. Her mother, Ellen, was a homemaker. Sadly, Ellen was killed by a drunk driver while out of town visiting relatives. My mother, Teri, raised me by herself working in a bucket factory. My father walked out on her after she revealed to him she was pregnant.

Following his wife's death, Richard decided to raise his only child in the small town.

Cindy and I were hometown sweethearts. You know, the whole star high school quarterback and the beautiful blonde head cheerleader. Yes, a small-town cliché. God, she was gorgeous. Her golden hair would shine like the heavens under the big lights on the field. When she was happy, her green eyes would brighten with such intensity that it was nearly like looking at the most exquisite of emeralds. I would stare in the mirror at my shaggy brown hair and dull, dark eyes, and think, how did I get someone as beautiful as Cindy?

Her dad set us up in this posh apartment and paid the rent for a year in order to give us time to find jobs. She wanted to be a Broadway star, and I was going to be a chef. But I gave up on my dream so that she could live hers.

She attended Columbia University majoring in Theater. I, on the other hand, had to work three part-time jobs to try and keep the bills paid. That meant nothing to me because I was with her.

On a whim, we registered for a marriage license and made it legal at a justice of the peace. It was the happiest time in my life. She was my everything. Then one day she came out of the bathroom with tears running down her cheeks, holding a white plastic stick. She was pregnant, and I was filled with more joy than I had ever felt. Cindy was filled with dread.

She had just been cast for a small part in a Broadway production.

"I can't be pregnant now!" she screamed as she sat in the middle of the floor.

"Babe, you can, and you will be a great mom," I said as I sat next to her pulling her into my arms.

"You can't honestly think I am going to keep it?" Her head popped up, and her puffy eyes shone with more anger than I had ever seen.

"Why wouldn't you?' I was so confused as to where the sweet, beautiful girl who talked of having children and had even picked out names for each of three she just knew she would have.

"Creek Hollis, I have just begun to live my dream, and now you want me to throw it all away?" She looked me straight in the eyes, and I couldn't see those emeralds anymore.

We talked, and she promised to think on it for a few days. About seven and a half months later, Lake Carter Hollis came into my life on Christmas day.

Cindy walked out two weeks later.

That was seven years ago.

She became a famous Broadway star who calls once or twice a month and sends gifts and cards for Christmas and birthdays. She never remarried and hasn't had any more kids.

I moved back home when Lake was about two years old. I needed help, and the reason Cindy's dad allowed me to stay in the apartment again was because he felt guilty about her walking away.

Now, I live in a small two-bedroom apartment attached to my mother's house.

"Creek!" I hear my name shouted behind me. I was lost in my memories again. I look at Joe as he bundles himself up to go out on this cold winter night. "Do you need a ride home?" he asks as he points the key fob at his KIA to remotely start it and warm up.

"No. But thanks, man," I respond as I pull my North Face coat on over my black hoodie.

"Creek, it's freezing out there," he says as I wrap my black scarf around my neck.

"I only have to walk six blocks. Plus, it gives me time to think."

We walk out the door, and I lock it once we're outside. Joe heads towards his car, already shivering, and I begin my trek. The wind has some whip to it as lashes my cheeks, but I don't mind it. I enjoy the peace I get when I walk. I like looking at all the decorations people have put up in their yards or on their houses.

Chapter 2.

As I walk through the back door removing all my layers of warmth, I can hear the television. Mom is watching a re-run of *In the Heat of the Night,* one of her favorite shows. When I've stripped down to my work clothes, I head toward the sound of the old tv show.

"How is he?" I ask as I take a seat on the old, worn-down, brown couch that Mom made me bring up from the basement.

"No fever. A little drained but nothing too bad." She begins packing her yarn and knitting needles in her bag to return to her side of the building. "Lois will be picking me up for work in the morning so you can use the car," she says as she kisses the top of my head.

"Thanks, Ma," I call out as she closes the door that separates the two living spaces. I sit for a few minutes before checking in on my boy.

I see the dimmed light from his bedside lamp that lets me know he's reading a book. Peeking through the two-inch crack between the door and its frame, Lake is laying on his belly reading a book.

I slowly open the door. "Hey, bud, whatcha reading?" I know it's *The Cat in the Hat* because it's his favorite.

"Hey, Dad. It's my favorite," he replies as he sits up, bringing the book with him, holding it up so I can see the cover.

"Well, it's time for bed. We have quite a drive in the morning and a long afternoon," I remind Lake as I pry the book out of his hand. "Did you brush your teeth?" He nods as I pick him up, hugging him tightly. His wiry arms wrap around my neck, and I just hold his frail, little body for a few minutes.

"Daddy, you're squeezing my life out." He tries to wiggle out of my embrace.

"You mean the life out of you?" We both giggle as I loosen my arms.

"That's what I said!" he exclaims as I hold him with one arm, pulling his Spiderman blanket and matching flat sheet back.

"Okay, big guy, it's sleep time." I lower him to his bed. Just before I tuck him in, I tickle his belly. His laugh is infectious. It is always beautiful to hear. Kissing his forehead, I turn to leave.

"Dad, we forgot to say our prayers!" Lake exclaims. I stop, turning back to him as he slides out of bed to kneel beside it. I join him as we clasp our hands and bow our heads.

"Dear God, thank you for this day. Thank you for giving me such a good Dad and nice Nana. She lets me have chocolate when I'm not feeling good. Please watch over them. Watch over Papa Richard and my mom. She is in Paris, so she needs some looking after. Help my dad find his true love. Help the doctors find a donor. Please make sure we safely make it to the hospital. Amen."

My heart breaks every night as my boy asks for a donor. He says the same prayer for me to find a true love every night, as well. I behold my son who has been through so much, yet has so much love in his heart. I kiss his head again before he nestles back into his bed.

Before I walk away, I stand in the doorway looking at this beautiful boy who once had blond hair. He inherited my eyes. Except for the dullness, his always seem so much brighter.

I'm not sure how much time I have with him. Lake has C-ALL (Childhood Acute Lymphoblastic Leukemia). He was diagnosed at four years old. He started running a fever and falling asleep quite often. Mom thought it might have been the flu in the beginning. But after of few days, my son got worse. We found a huge lump under his armpit, and I knew in my heart there was something wrong. So, we rushed him to the nearest hospital about twenty minutes out of town.

After all the typical and routine tests were completed, the head pediatrician and a pediatric oncologist were called in, and they took us to a private room and broke the devastating news. I looked over at my mother who was sobbing in disbelief as I was broken hearted. They said it was in its pretty early stages and wanted to start chemotherapy as soon as possible. I felt like I was in some sort of alternate universe. They had Lake transferred to the children's hospital about two and a half hours away. We were there for a long while, and I watched my rambunctious little guy turn into a mere shell of himself. His hair fell out; he couldn't hold anything down. My soul shattered until the news came that his cancer was in remission, and he slowly began to return to my healthy little guy.

About two weeks ago, the day after Thanksgiving, my soul had been destroyed once again when another lump formed in his groin and one on his neck. We were informed the cancer was back and aggressive. He needs a bone marrow transplant; however, I am not a match—I had been tested the first go around. Neither were my mom or Mr. Grove. I have no clue if Cindy has been tested. She's been out of the country for about a year now. I called when the cancer returned and had to leave a message. It's been a few weeks, and I've heard nothing.

Chapter 3

As the alarm begins to screech, I reach over to turn it off. I barely slept as all the what-ifs ran through my mind. *What if they don't find a donor? What if they do find one but his body rejects it?*

I sit up in bed and run my hands over my face. My legs swing over the edge of the bed, hitting the frigid wood floor. I hurriedly look for my slippers that are lodged under the bed. Once the fuzzy warmth hits my feet, I make my way to the bathroom.

After starting the shower, I turn toward the mirror as I pull the white t-shirt I slept in over my head. The orange ribbon tattoo (the symbol for Leukemia) that sets just above my heart is still as bright as the day I got it—the day we got the news that Lake was in remission. I run my hand over the image as I close my eyes, trying to keep the tears that threaten to spill at bay. I have prayed...no...begged God to spare my little boy. He doesn't deserve what he has been put through, nor what is yet to come. I stand there and pray for a donor. Lifting my head, I gaze at the now fogged mirror.

I pick out some clothes and get myself dressed. After brushing my teeth and combing my hair, I head to the kitchen to get some coffee brewing before waking up Lake. But when I turn into the doorway, I see my mom sitting at the tiny table that's set in front a small window.

"Good morning," she says as she stands, grabbing a mug and pouring steamy hot, brown liquid into it.

She hands me the drink that warms my hands and settles back into looking out at the freshly fallen snow. She's worried. Hopefully, today, we get some news that they found a donor.

We sit in silence for a brief moment before she stands as her best friend Lois knocks on my door. My mom begins to put on her coat as she walks towards the door. I follow behind.

"Hey, Creek," Lois whispers as she pulls me into her arms. I soak in her embrace before kissing her cheek.

"Son, make sure you call me if there's any news," Mom says as she gives me a sorrowful look.

"I will," I answer as they walk out the door.

Entering Lake's room, I catch him sitting up reading. "Hey, bud, time to get dressed. Do you know what you want to wear?"

Lake gets out of bed, opens his closet, and pulls out his favorite blue sweats and sweatshirt. I search his dresser and retrieve a white t-shirt and some socks.

Once he is fully clothed, I ask if he'd like some toast. He nods as he goes to brush his teeth.

When his toast is madee, I grab a bottle of water out of the refrigerator, placing them on the table. Lake sits in the seat his grandmother was occupying earlier so he can look at the snow.

"Hey, bud, I'm going to start the car to warm it up and brush it off." He nods, his gaze not leaving the window.

I slip on my boots and exit the house, the cold air hitting me hard. I walk as fast as I can to the car, shivering as the chill runs through my jeans and blue flannel shirt. As I pull the door open, I hurriedly stick the key in, turning it over. Once the engine roars to life, I feel around the backseat until I connect with the cold plastic of the snow brush. While grabbing it, I notice Mom's bright pink mittens sitting on the passenger seat and put them on. I slide out of the car and start removing all the snow from the windows. Hearing a tap on the kitchen's window pane, I look up to see Lake laughing at the gloves I have on. I smile at him, collect some snow, forming it into a ball, and throw it at the window.

*****

We pull up to the valet stand at Children's Hospital; the circular fifteen-story building with reflective glass on the windows always has me wondering who cleans them, and how much do they get paid?

I jump out of the car, grabbing Lake's blue Superman backpack filled with snacks, books, and medication as the valet walks up to the passenger side. He opens the door for my son. I prefer this type of parking; it makes it easier to maneuver. I hate circling the layers of lots for a spot.

Once we make it inside the hospital, I begin to help Lake take his winter gear off. "Dad, look, Dave is here today!" He is super excited. Dave works at the security desk. When little guy was doing chemo a few years ago, they had become great friends. And, every year since then, a book and card come addressed to Lake from Dave. We send him cards, as well.

After I get my son's coat and hat off, he runs straight to the security guard. "Hey, Dave!" he calls out and runs and jumps up to the big, burly man.

"Hey, Lake! How's my little friend?" Dave inquires as he carries him back towards me.

"My cancer's back." Lake shows a sad face as he hugs tightly to his friend. I see a sullen look fall across Dave's face.

"Hello, Creek," the man says as he reaches his free hand out to me. I see the question in his eyes, and I just shake my head. He has worked at this hospital for many years; I'm sure he's seen much heartache. He holds tight to Lake before he puts him back on his feet, then turns his back as I see his hand go up to his face, wiping what I assume are tears from his eyes.

"We got to go now, Dave. I will stop and see you before I leave," Lake says as he grabs my hand, pulling me towards the elevators.

Chapter 4.

The elevator dings, letting us know we have made it to the ninth floor. Oncology. The doors open to a huge waiting room with brightly colored chairs. Ballerinas, cowboys, superhero pictures adorn the walls. When I begin to walk out of the elevator as Lake darts out in front of me yelling, "Papa Richard!" I walk over to where they are standing.

"Creek, good to see you," Richard says holding his hand out to me. After we shake, I ask him why he is here. "Dr. Courtney called me and asked if I'd attend this morning's appointment," he replies as Lake hops in the seat next to him.

"She didn't happen to say why?" I look at him as he gazes at his grandson. He shakes his head.

I check us in at the desk then sit quietly while Richard reads Lake one of books from his backpack. About fifteen minutes later Dr. Courtney comes over to where we are sitting.

"Good morning, Lake. Creek, we won't be in an exam room today; instead, we are going down to the seventh floor and use a conference room. Mr. Grove, you, too." She holds Lake's hand as they stroll towards the bank of elevators ahead of us.

The elevator car stops on our designated floor, and we exit, turning right then walking down a long hallway with doors on each side. Dr. Courtney leads us to the end of the hall and opens a door with a sign that says, Conference Room A. There are already two other people sitting at the small rectangle wood table. As we enter, a man with graying hair cut military style and dressed in a blue button-down dress shirt and gray slacks stands.

My son's doctor makes introductions all around. "Dr. Michael Stokes, I would like you to meet our little patient Lake Hollis, his dad, Creek, and grandfather Richard Grove. This young lady across the table is Nurse Kelly Marshall. They have been briefed on Lake's diagnosis." We all shake hands and take a seat at the table.

"Let me start by saying we have found a donor," Dr. Stokes says as he makes his way over to Lake, mussing his hair. His face brightens the room when he gives a big toothy grin as my heart starts beating fast, and I fill with joy. "So, we need to begin chemo and/or radiation therapy to start eradicating all those bad cells. This is what we call conditioning."

Dr. Courtney stands, and so does the cute brunette nurse with caring brown eyes. My stomach had lurched at the thought of what the chemo will do to him.

"But before all of that, Dr. Stokes will run some tests. He needs to assess Lake's condition. Then he will need to implant a long thin tube called an intravenous catheter into a large vein. Sometimes it's put in the chest, but for someone Lake's age, we think the neck is best. This will be a central line for Dr. Stokes to use to infuse the stem cells from the donor. It will also be used for medicine and blood if needed," explains Nurse Kelly, then she crouches down next to Lake. "Also, I will be his main nurse through the whole process."

"Now, I'm sure, Mr. Grove, you're wondering why I asked you here. After the tests are finished, they will help us determine if Lake will need one or two weeks of conditioning. We want him to be as safe and comfortable as possible during this time period, keeping him as secluded from bacteria as possible, thus decreasing his chance of infection. So, the hospital has chosen to implement a new program where our nurse will stay at the patient's home and administer the chemotherapy. This helps him to acclimate better, and his father will still be able to go to work. And if Lake feels up to it, continue his homeschooling. Since this will be considered a trial run, it will cost you nothing. Given that Mr. Grove handles the bills, we thought it pertinent he be here," Dr. Courtney says as she hands us each a pamphlet.

"So, Nurse Kelly will stay at my house?" Lake asks with excitement.

"Yes," the doctor answers. "If your father agrees to the trial. We feel it will be easier than bringing him back and forth to do his conditioning, and it will also cut his chances of infection."

I am reading over the pamphlet, and it sounds so much better than driving him two hours each way. A puking kid does not make for a good car ride.

"When do we do the testing and assessment?" I ask, looking over at my boy who is about to go through hell to fight for his life.

"How about tomorrow? We will get him admitted, start the blood work, then insert the tube. Hopefully, we'll have you home the day after tomorrow or possibly the day after that." Dr. Courtney appears excited. I'm glad I have a few days off.

I look to Lake who is grinning and nodding his head at me. "Well, the boss there says yes, so let's get this started," I say as Lake points his thumbs in at himself.

"Yep. I'm the boss!"

Chapter 5.

After all the pre-transplant testing has been completed, and the intravenous catheter has been inserted into Lake's neck, we are finally back home with instructions for cleaning and caring for the area around the tube. They gave me a surgical dressing that they called CD-1000, so he can shower and not worry about getting the site infected.

My son will do one weeks' worth of aggressive chemo, and if this protocol works, then his transplant will be on the twenty-fourth of December. If the next set of blood tests shows not a lot of progress, then he will do another week of conditioning, and his transplant will be held off an additional week. Either way, we'll be spending Christmas and his birthday or the New Year at the children's hospital. But hey, if it's going to make my boy better then I don't much care.

The nurse will be here Sunday to start the chemo. That's three days from now. Mom suggested we take the burgundy rocker-recliner from her living room to put in Lakes room so I can sleep in it at night to be close to him during his treatment. She also went out and purchased new linens for my bed so that Nurse Kelly has somewhere comfortable to sleep while staying here.

I thought my sheets were just fine, but apparently, they smell like man...whatever that means. Now, my once masculine bed is all girly with sheets adorned with pink roses and a pink fleece blanket to match.

"Has Cindy called you back?" Mom asks as she puts the last bleachy scrub to my bathroom sink. We have always cleaned with bleach to minimize the germs Lake was exposed to, but Mom has overdone it. So much so that I had to open some windows, so we wouldn't choke on the fumes, and it's freezing outside.

"No, Mom. I'm sure she will. I left her a message about having found a donor."

She just shakes her head as she tries not to show me her anger. The woman holds great disdain for Cindy. I mean, some people would say it's justly warranted, and I'm always being asked why I don't share those same feelings. They can't seem to understand why I have allowed her contact with our son after she left. Especially since she didn't make contact until six weeks later. I have explained that no matter what Cindy has done, she will always be Lake's mother. I feel that, in some way, it was me that drove her to leave by attempting to force motherhood on her. I mean, I didn't demand she keeps him or force her to get pregnant, but admit I was a little selfish in wanting the tiny human we had created. I thought it would be the glue to hold us together forever.

Even though my heart shattered when she left, I have forgiven her because I don't want to spend my life bitter and angry over a situation I couldn't control. What kind of man would I be to show any hatred towards my son's mother? What would that teach him? Not to trust women? To never let anyone close to him that could break his heart? Or have him grow up to be bitter as well? No, I wasn't going to be *that* guy.

"What kind of mother doesn't call to check on her kid? A worthless one if you ask me," Mom mumbles under her breath, walking into the kitchen.

"Please don't talk like that around Lake." I grab my favorite black and white #1 Dad mug from the drying rack next to the sink. Mom pours the fresh coffee she made in it for me.

"You know my feelings about that woman. I didn't like her when you were dating. That's why you got married all sneakily. You knew I would never have approved." Mom is right I didn't need the grief she would have given me about marrying Cindy. I loved that girl with everything I had.

"Yes, Mother, I know. You only remind me of my mistake every other day," I say rolling my eyes.

"The only good thing that came out of that debacle is Lake. So, I will give her props for giving us him." We sit silently sipping our coffee. I look at the time on the microwave. I need to get to work.

Taking one more sip of the warm liquid, I kiss mom on top of her head. "Love you, Ma," I say as I exit the kitchen.

*****

It's not a bad day for a walk. The sun is shining; however, it's only thirty degrees, and the wind is lightly blowing. I keep a steady pace just trying to clear my mind. My phone begins to buzz in my pocket, and I take my glove off to reach in and grab it. I look at the screen, and Cindy's name is there.

"Hey, Cindy," I say as I slow my steps to almost snail-like.

"I got your message about Lake. Sorry, cell service is spotty here. What's the plan of action?" I hear true concern in her tone.

"Ultimately, the bone marrow transplant. But first, he must endure a week of chemo. They call it conditioning." I stop walking.

"So, is there a date for the transplant?" she asks. "Yes, the transplant is happening on Christmas Eve if this week goes well. Will you be back in the states by then?" My last question came out a little angrier than I intended it to.

"I'm trying to get back there in time for Christmas. Creek, how are you holding up?" I am a little taken aback by her concern for me.

"I'm good. I'm on my way to work so, call me and let me know when you'll be getting in to town." Neither of us hangs up right away.

"I will, Creek," is the last thing she says before I hear the click letting me know she ended the call.

I stand in the same spot for a few minutes before I finish my walk to work. As I travel my repetitive route to work, I realize something; I didn't experience the butterflies in my stomach that I used to when we spoke. The same butterflies I felt the first time I asked her out. I had still been getting them, even after seven years of not being together, but not today. I guess some part of me had always held out hope that she would come back and tell me she made a big mistake, and we could be a family again.

I haven't even dated anyone since high school.

It had only been her.

God, that's sad.

Chapter 6.

A medical company came yesterday to deliver the supplies Nurse Kelly will need to administer the chemotherapy to Lake. My living room has an IV pole, boxes of IV tubing, gloves, and some other things.

It's 7:30 in the morning. Lake woke me up at 6:30 so we could be ready for our visitor. Now, he is sitting at the kitchen table in his favorite spot eating his breakfast when a red Ford Freestyle Minivan pulls in.

"Dad, she's here!" He jumps from his seat, excitedly racing to put on his boots and coat.

"Lake! Lake! Stop!" I run behind him. He is in his Transformers pajamas, hurrying towards the back of the vehicle that the nurse has just opened.

"Good morning, gentlemen," Nurse Kelly says with a bright smile and arms full of more medical boxes.

"Lake, go inside. You're still in your pajamas; you'll catch your death," Mom sighs as she approaches us. "Hi, I'm Teri Hollis, Lake's grandmother," she says as she turns my son around to get him back in the house.

"Here, let me help you with something." I grab the boxes from her arms and take them back to my apartment. I place the boxes she brought along with the ones that are already occupying my living room and head back out. She is pulling two rolling suitcases and carrying a laptop bag on her shoulder. I take the luggage from her, helping her get to the warmth of the inside.

After Nurse Kelly has had a hot cup of coffee and Lake is showered, it's time to begin his conditioning. We decided that he would be more relaxed in the recliner in his room. I move the 22-inch flat screen from my bedroom into his, so he can watch his DVDs.

When he's all hooked up and comfortable, I show my guest her sleeping accommodations. She puts her personal belongings in the room and joins me in the kitchen.

"Do you have wi-fi?" she asks as she pulls out her laptop and iPad. I nod as I pull the small piece of paper off the fridge with the account's information on it. "I will be logging his vitals, any reactions, and any other information needed into a chart that will be seen by Dr. Courtney and Dr. Stokes. I will also be skyping with Dr. Courtney once a day so that she can talk to Lake. If an infection does begin, they have set up a plan to have Lake medevacked to Children's Hospital ASAP. I have meds with me for any nausea he may incur, and of course, you've seen me give him Children's Motrin beforehand to help with any fever or discomfort he may begin to feel during this treatment." As the nurse is speaking, she types in the vitals she took before hooking him up.

Mom joins us in the kitchen. "So, Nurse Kelly, how many hours will he have to do these treatments a day?" she asks as she takes a seat at the small table.

"Please, just call me Kelly. They'll last about five hours as long as his body can tolerate it. We need to kill off the existing harmful cells to get him ready for the new ones that will be entering his body during the transplant," she explains before exiting the kitchen.

"I think we should celebrate Christmas and his birthday early," Mom suggests as she stares out the window. "I want Lake to able to enjoy his gifts. We don't need to throw a party for his birthday; I'm sure he won't be up to eating cake and ice cream. But let him open his gifts. Maybe the day before Christmas Eve since he'll be checking into the hospital that day. If he's feeling up to it, I would like to get the tree up and decorated." Usually, the tree would go up a few days after Thanksgiving, but with the news of Lake's leukemia returning, we haven't been in the holiday spirit.

"Sounds good. Make sure he gets on the laptop and does some school work." Mom looks at me with a put-on smile. She is worried this transplant won't take. I have that fear, too, but I also know my son is a fighter.

I also believe that whatever happens, I will always be thankful for the time I've had or will have with him. "I'll grab some wrapping paper on my way to the diner, so we can get the stuff hidden in your bedroom closet wrapped." I place an arm around Mom's shoulders and squeeze her. She pats my hand then holds her hand on top of mine as we silently watch the white flakes fall through the frosted window.

*****

The work hours seemed to drag along as I worried about how my son was feeling. I called home a few times just to check in. The clock finally displays nine o'clock, and I all but run out of the place. At the last minute, I remember I'm supposed to get some wrapping paper and walk towards Mr. Hopper's Five & Dime, praying he is still open. I can see the lights are still on, so I race down the block just in time to see Mr. Hopper turning the open sign to closed. He smiles at me, though, and re-opens the door.

"Creek, I saw you hightailing towards the store. What is so important?" I walk towards a display filled with all kinds of wrapping paper.

"I was supposed to buy some wrapping paper before my shift at the diner but got sidetracked and forgot." I chuckle.

"Well, I assume it's for wrapping Lake's gifts? I saved a couple rolls with those Transporter characters the boys seem to like," he says as he walks towards the back of the shop.

"You mean, Transformers?" He stops.

"That's what I said. Transporters." I laugh. *I'll just let him think he's right.*

He comes back to where he left me. "Here you go. I saved two rolls, one red and one blue." As I reach towards my back pocket to grab my wallet, Mr. Hopper grabs my arm. "No charge, Creek. That little boy deserves to smile. We heard he'll be receiving a bone marrow transplant for Christmas. I know my Transporter wrapping paper isn't much, but if it gives him a little happiness, then, well, that's payment enough." He puts the wrapping paper in my hand, and I thank him. Nothing better than small town living.

Chapter 7.

When I came home from work last night, Mom and Kelly were drinking cocoa and shooting the breeze at the kitchen table. I walked into the room to get a glass of water and let them know I was home as I handed Mom the wrapping paper before I went to check on Lake. He was curled into a ball sound asleep in the recliner. I picked him up and put him in his bed, and placed a slight kiss on his forehead. I stood there for a few minutes silently saying a prayer. I hope it's heard.

Waking up to somewhat whispered giggles this morning would annoy most people, but to me, it makes me happy. It means that Lake is doing well with his treatment. I peek my head out from under the blanket I turned into a nice warm cocoon last night. I see Kelly and Lake watching something on his tablet and assume it's one of those prank videos he seems to be obsessed with on YouTube. I stretch, letting them know I am awake as I poke my head out from under the blanket.

"Dad, your awake!" my son exclaims as he sets down the tablet and leaps over Kelly to jump into my arms.

"Morning, son. I see you're feeling well." I tickle him just to hear his infectious laughter. "Have you had breakfast yet?" I ask throwing him over my shoulder.

"Yes, Kelly made me a boiled egg. She said I needed the protein." I look at the curvy, dark-haired woman who has a smile that almost makes you forget all your woes.

"Well, I guess she would know best being a nurse and all. How about a quick shower before treatment," I say with a wink. "So, I work a short shift this afternoon; maybe we should put the tree up afterwards?" Lake begins beating on my back, chanting yes.

I sit him in the recliner as Kelly puts the dressing over his catheter. "Now, hurry, Dad needs a shower, too." He grabs his change of clothes as we walk into the bathroom.

I finally jump in the nice, hot shower to help relax my stiff muscles caused by sleeping in the recliner. Dressing quickly, I then join Kelly at the table where she is typing on her laptop. "Everything all good?" I ask as I begin filling my mug.

"Yes, his vitals are good. Today being the second day may bring on some nausea and muscle aches, but I'll keep them monitored. He is a strong boy; I think he'll do well. If he is feeling okay later on when you all are doing your tree, I may go into town to give you guys some family time," she says closing the laptop.

"You don't have to do that. Stay, Mom makes rice crispy treats, cocoa, and popcorn to put on a string for the tree. Then we pick a movie, usually *A Christmas Story*, to end the night." I am not a fan of the movie, but Mom and Lake love it. She looks at me with a smile then nods letting me know she likes the idea of joining us. I like that idea, too.

*****

For only a four-hour shift, I am beat. The diner was a non-stop barrage of shoppers. We had mostly to-go orders, but they were huge. Most people don't want to cook after spending the day searching for the perfect gift for the ones they love. I did most of my shopping before Thanksgiving; therefore, I'm just waiting on a few things to be delivered. Lake doesn't ever ask for a lot, so what he does ask for I try to get him. Thanks to Mom not charging me rent, I can afford those things.

As I walk up the driveway, I grab the snow shovel kept beside the house and begin throwing the heavy snow to the side so people can get in and out without getting stuck. Before I know it, I've shoveled our sidewalk, driveway, and both neighbors on each side of us. My fingers are frozen numb, and I think a few of my toes fell off, or they are just frozen solid, as well.

When I enter the house, the smell of my mom's homemade chicken soup, popcorn, and coffee fill the air. I hear *The Little Drummer Boy* playing on the radio in the living room. *This is what the holiday is supposed to smell and sound like.* I stop off in the kitchen and lift the lid off the pot I know is the soup, wafting the steam towards my nose, deeply inhaling the scent of deliciousness. I pour myself some of warm, delicious-smelling java and make my way to the living room. All the boxes that had been scattered everywhere are now neatly stacked in a corner, and a six-foot Spruce is nicely standing against the one window in the room.

"Wow, it smells like the forest in here. Where did this tree come from?" I ask as I take a sip from the mug that is warming my hands.

"Papa brought it. Isn't it huge, Dad?" Lake and Kelly are sitting on the couch where they have already strung what looks to be about four bowls of popcorn, give or take what they haven't eaten themselves.

"Yeah, son, it sure is." I walk over to the chair Mom is sitting in as she tries to untangle the Christmas lights.

"Damn it, Creek, every year I ask you to wrap the lights around the spindle, and every year I have to untangle them. It's exhausting," she says throwing the ball of lights she was just holding.

"And every year you get flustered, turn red, and use swear words. It's like a Christmas tradition. You're always saying we need to have a tradition." The room erupts into giggles but not from Mom.

"Only a lazy man would say that," she retorts, picking the ball up for one more try. I see Kelly cover her mouth, holding back a laugh after my mother's reply.

Lake and Kelly hang the popcorn garland they have just finished and wrap it around the tree. I have untangled two sets of lights, put them on the tree, and plugged them in. Mom calls out that the soup is ready, and we all file into the kitchen where she already has bowls filled up and a plate full of homemade buttermilk biscuits. There are only three chairs at the table, so I give Kelly mine as I lean against the counter holding the bowl of yumminess.

"Did you do some work for school today?" I ask Lake before shoveling a big spoonful noodles into my mouth.

"Yes, Dad. I did some math, some spelling, and read a book." I watch as my son only sips the broth wondering if he is feeling queasy.

"Good. Is your tummy not feeling good?" I set my bowl down to see if he is running a fever. "A little. I love Nana's soup, so I will just drink the juice, if that's okay?" I nod my head, and we resume eating.

"I have something for your tummy if you need it, Lake," Kelly says getting up from her seat and leaving the room. When she returns, she has a bottle in her hand. "You can take this pink stuff first to see if it helps, or I can give you a shot of Zofran?" Lake sits and think for a second and picks the pink stuff (Pepto).

"Geesh, this stuff is gross! Maybe I should have took the shot. Yuck." Lake wipes his mouth and ingests a hearty gulp of his water in hopes of the nasty taste leaving. We all laugh at the faces he is making. The kid is hilarious.

Chapter 8.

Lake went to bed early. He wasn't in the mood for a movie, but he wanted to put the angel on the top of the tree because it's his job. Mom tucked him in, and Kelly took his vitals as we skyped Dr. Courtney. She asked Lake how he was feeling. He told her his tummy felt like he was on a rollercoaster. She asked if he'd like Kelly to give him the shot and his exact words were, "I would rather show Kelly one of my butt cheeks than taste that pink slime again." He was informed that it could be given through his tube, so Nurse Kelly would not have to see his butt. So, now, along with the Children's Motrin, he will get a small dose of the anti-nausea medication before his treatment. Other than today's tummy upset, Dr. Courtney says everything looks good. She wants the nurse to take some blood the day after tomorrow that will be picked up and brought back to the hospital so they can see if the chemo is making any progress.

We finished the tree, Kelly and me. I washed the dirty dishes and made some cocoa for us. "Want to watch a movie?" I ask as I carry in two steaming cups of chocolatey goodness.

"Sure, anything but *A Christmas Story*," she states as she releases her hair from the bun she had it in, and it falls, cascading over her shoulders.

"Oh, you can't possibly despise a holiday cult classic such as *A Christmas Story*. I think that is like against some Christmas law." I let out a laugh as I feel a relief fall on my heart.

"Well, sometimes you just got to live on the edge," she says blowing on her cocoa before taking a sip.

"Thank god. I really hate that movie. What would you like to watch?" I ask as I point to the shelves that house my unhealthy DVD obsession. Most people have Netflix; I prefer to own my favorites.

"How about *Die Hard*? That *should be* a required Christmas cult classic," she says matter-of-factly. I power up the player, grab the case that houses the *Die-Hard* DVD, taking it out and putting it into the machine. She is sitting on one end of the couch as I take my seat at the other. We settle in for some John McClane action.

Once the movie ends, Kelly goes to check on Lake while I take our dirty cocoa mugs to the kitchen. After Kelly has finished, she joins me in the kitchen and opens up her laptop to enter my son's vitals.

"Would you like another cup of cocoa?" I ask before washing and putting away our mugs.

"No, I will get a bottle of water from the refrigerator. Thank you, though." She removes her water then sits back down. After my task is done, I grab myself a bottle and join her.

"So, Kelly, are you from Ohio?" I open my bottle, taking a big drink.

"Yes, from Sandusky," she says closing her screen. "I recently moved to Cincinnati after finishing my clinical courses and was hired at the Children's Hospital." She lifts her legs and sits Indian-style in the chair. She is tiny; curvy, but tiny.

"What made you want to work with ill kids? Some terminal. I'm having a rough time trying not to fall apart in front of my son; I couldn't imagine getting close to those poor kids then having to watch them suffer." I cringe at the thought, remembering what I felt when Lake was diagnosed the first time and watching him go through the chemo.

"I've only been with the hospital a few months, so I haven't worked with a lot of the kids. But my decision to become a pediatric nurse for children with cancer came from watching my childhood friend go from a healthy, high school cheerleading captain to a bed-ridden and frail scared girl.

"Beth was my neighbor and best friend since I was two. We did everything together, from starting kindergarten to the cheerleading squad. She was beautiful, tall, blonde, and smart. I was her total opposite.

"One day, we were at practice, and Beth got a cut that wouldn't stop bleeding. I remember sitting in the waiting room with her siblings for what we thought would be her getting stitched up to her mom emerging from the ER with tears cascading down her face. When the doctors had a hard time stopping the bleeding, they ran some tests and found out Beth had leukemia.

"I knew what the disease was and knew it was bad. I begged my mom to homeschool me, so I could be there for Beth during her chemo and help her through the effects of the treatment. We were told that the drugs were doing nothing but slowing the progression of the cancer, and it was just wearing her down. Faced with the doctor's prognosis. Beth decided she wanted to live what time she had left without the all the side effects that chemotherapy brought with it. I stayed with her, held her, and then watched her take her last breath only six months after her diagnosis. She was only sixteen, and I recognized then that I wanted to help kids with cancer. I will be applying to med school next year to become a pediatric cancer specialist." Her eyes shimmer from the tears threatening to fall.

"Beth was lucky to have a friend like you by her side 'til the end." I grab her hand that is resting on the table top and give it a squeeze. She squeezes me back before I move my hand away.

Chapter 9.

I went to bed thinking about Kelly's story and how hard all that must have been for a teenage girl to see and go through. I crawled into bed with Lake so that I could hold him close. I've witnessed the effects cancer treatments have on a child's body. On my son's first round, I watched his body slowly get frail. I was so scared of losing him that I begged God to give all of Lake's pain and sickness to me; I was bigger and stronger. But through God's grace, he got better. I thank Him every day for not taking my boy from me. Now, I'm back to praying that he doesn't leave this earth.

"Dad. Dad! You're squeezing my life out!" I feel his body squirm. "Dad, why are you in my bed? It's not big enough for us both," he says as I loosen my hold. "What are you, too big to share a bed with your dad now? I remember a time when you would sneak into mine in the middle of the night." I open my eyes to see Kelly standing next to the bed smiling at our exchange.

"Morning, gentlemen. Lake, time to take your Motrin and Zofran. Do you want toast or maybe some fruit salad?" I look at her puzzled because when I went to bed, there was no fruit in the house. I had a grocery list made up and put it on the fridge door that I had intended on getting today. "I got up a few hours ago, came in here, and well, you two were sound asleep. I saw your list, so I decided to go to the 24-hour grocery store a town over and do the shopping." She shrugs as she wraps the blood pressure cuff around Lake's little wrist.

"Please tell me how much you spent, and I will get your money back to you," I say as I slide to the end of the twin bed.

"Don't worry about it. So, which is it, buddy, fruit or warm bread?" She looks at my little boy with a raised brow after she removes the machine from his wrist.

"Fruit!" he yells as he rushes towards the bathroom, slamming the door. I laugh as I stretch.

"Thanks for doing the shopping. I'll write you a check for whatever you spent." I look over at the nurse whose face is turning shades of pink, remembering I have on grey sweats and no shirt.

"I, huh...like your tattoo," she sputters out, pulling her shirt down enough to show me her orange ribbon. Same side, same spot.

After Kelly got Lake all hooked up in the chair, I fired up the laptop for him to do some schoolwork. I don't have to work today, so I think if Lake's feeling up to it, we can watch some movies and eat leftover soup. I gather up all of our dirty laundry and go down the basement wash them. I stop in the living room where Kelly is reading on her iPad to see if she needs anything washed as well.

"I'm going to do a couple of loads of laundry; anything you want to throw in?" She says no, never looking up from whatever it is that she's engulfed in. "What are you reading, medical stuff?" I ask as I set the basket of clothes down. Her cheeks turn that shade of pink they were this morning.

"No. Just a book," she replies, attempting to hide her embarrassment.

"Well, that 'just a book' has your face a pretty shade of pink." I laugh as I pick my basket back up.

After getting the laundry squared away, Lake asked if we could watch the movie in his room because he wasn't feeling well. Since it was his choice, we watched that *wretched* movie. Now my dreams will be filled with the words, "You'll shoot your eye out." But we pushed through and laughed when we were supposed to. Now we're watching *Gremlins*. Lake asked Kelly to sit with him on his bed, and I am in the recliner. Occasionally, I look over at them both with their eyes drooping almost closed. My son is snuggled into Kelly's side as she was softly rubbing his head. The last time I glanced over, though, they were both asleep. I could feel sleep claiming me as well, but to see my son relaxing with a smile on his face is truly a sight to behold.

I wake up to the sounds of Kelly doing her thing. Looking over at my boy, he is looking a little peaked. "Son, how are you feeling?" I jump up out of the chair that has been serving as a bed for me.

"He's got a small fever, but nothing too major. It was kind of expected before now. We'll keep an eye on it, and if it goes over a hundred, we will worry then." She gives a smile that says I should believe her and leaves me with a feeling of relief. I walk out to the living room where I see that Mom has wrapped and packed all the presents under the tree. I go to grab me a mug full of liquid energy and see a note on the fridge.

Creek,

Cindy called, but you didn't hear your phone, so she called me. She is still trying to rearrange her schedule to be here in time for the transplant. Soon as she gets the flight info, she'll call again.

MOM

Kelly joins me. "Is Cindy his mom?" she asks as she sits down. I nod as I take the seat across from her. "Where is she?" I tell her about my life with the mother of my child. She has a look of pity, or maybe it's sympathy.

"Oh, wow. So, you've raised Lake on your own. Wasn't she around when he was first diagnosed?" I answer her with a simple no.

"I'm not mad at her for her choices. She gave me Lake. He was the greatest gift I have ever been given." I smile at the nurse who is ready to weep buckets of tears.

"Creek, you are a great man and a fabulous dad." She grabs my hand, holding it in hers. Her hand feels like it was made just to fit into mine.

Chapter 10.

It's been a crazy few days. The diner has been non-stop, I've worked some double shifts due to the rush of people. My nights after work have been spent watching movies and talking to Kelly. Lake's fever stayed for a day then subsided, thank god. We need him to be healthy for his procedure.

Today is the day Kelly will draw blood to see if the treatments are doing their job. I've been praying every night for my son to get what he needs, to be a healthy young man. Kelly has been fantastic with him. She helps him with his school work and reads to him at night. I'm glad she was chosen to do this trial run with us.

I put my snow gear on to shovel the snow that fell last night. The sun is shining. It makes the outside so bright with the rays of sunlight beaming off the freshly fallen snow. I take time to look around and can't believe I've missed all the messages for Lake that people are displaying in their yards and writing in fake snow on their windows. Some say, "God bless you, Lake." Others, "You got this, Lake." One message said, "Lake, you are in our prayers." I walk up and down the middle of the street looking at the houses with tears freezing on my cheeks. Grabbing my phone, I take pictures of each message to show my son what community really means. I run into the house, not bothering to take my coat or boots off. As I pass the kitchen, I holler for Mom and Kelly to follow me. I pause the movie Lake is watching and tell the ladies to gather around the chair, so we can all see the love. I begin the slideshow, and the room fills with tears.

*****

We've been on edge waiting for the results of the blood test since the Lab Core vehicle left the driveway four hours ago. We've watched movies, played board games, and now, Lake is napping as we, the adults, sit in the living room in a deafening silence sipping coffee. I understand things like this take a while, but this is nerve-wracking.

A loud ring from Kelly's iPad makes every one of us jump. She grabs the thing and answers. "Are the Hollis's with you?" I hear Dr. Courtney ask.

"Yes, yes, they're right here." Mom and I stand behind Kelly so the doctor can see us. "So, the results of the blood work show..." She just breaks off, and my heart stops beating. "That the conditioning is working!" She almost screams it as we all let out the breathes we had been holding. "Therefore, the procedure will be in three days' time. Kelly, let's hold off on treatment tomorrow, but I'd like you to stay there to monitor Lake. Okay, everyone, see you on the 24th to get our young one admitted." We all thank her and take in a refreshing sigh of relief.

"We will do Christmas tomorrow morning," Mom says. I nod.

"Do you just do a Christmas celebration, or do you combine his birthday and Christmas?" Kelly asks as she sets her iPad down.

"What we do is combine them. His gifts are all Christmas ones, but Mom makes him a birthday cake for after dinner. His mom focuses more on his birthday. She has balloons and gifts wrapped in birthday wrapping paper delivered." She looks at me with a questioning look.

"Delivered?" she asks.

"Yes, Ms. Cindy has engagements that seem to be more important than making time to come see her only son," Mom chimes in. I give her a disapproving look.

"My mom isn't very fond of Cindy as you may have noticed." I chuckle as I say it.

Kelly mentioned she wanted to go to a couple of the shops in town and do a little shopping, so I decided to join her. There was a watch I'd seen that I wanted to get for Mom and a few things I thought Lake would like. Mom was going to help the boy with some schoolwork since he probably wasn't going to feel like doing anything for a little while.

Kelly went her way to the boutiques, and I made my way to the jeweler and toy store. We met back at the Country Kitchen to grab a bite to eat about an hour or so later. I found us a booth near the back.

Mia, one of the waitresses' saunters—yes, saunters—over to us. "Well, hey there, Creek, what can I get for ya?" She never once looks at Kelly.

"Hey, Mia, I'll have a cheeseburger with everything, some onion rings, and a coke. Kelly, what will you have?" Mia turns to her with a look of disdain and maybe a little jealousy.

"I think I'll have what he's having. It sounds delicious." Kelly closes the menu that she was looking over.

"Oh, you think that's wise? That's a lot of calories, and hun, you look like you need less calories in your diet," she sneers. Before either one of us can say anything, Ms. Mary, the owner, stalks over to us.

"Mia, I didn't just hear you say something rude to this beautiful, young lady, did I? Give me their ticket. I will handle their order, personally. You, my dear, are on coffee detail. Make sure there is fresh coffee in every pot and cup." Mia hands our order over to the sweet lady, and she rips it up. "Creek, your meal is on Mia. Ms., I apologize for my employee. You see, she has been eyeballing this young man since she started here, and he hasn't given her a second look." She gives us an endearing smile.

"Ms. Mary, this is Kelly Marshall. She is Lake's nurse. She's been staying with us so he could do his chemo at home," I tell her.

"How is the lad?" she asks.

"He's doing incredibly well, all things considered. His conditioning worked, and in three days, he will get his bone marrow transplant." Kelly speaks up this time.

"Oh, Creek, that is wonderful! We have been praying for him and your family."

I take out my phone to show her the support from all the neighbors. By the last picture, she is brought to tears just like we were.

"That is truly amazing. Creek, you take off as much time as you need. Let me go put your order in so you all can eat." She slides out of the booth where she was seated beside me, reaches into the pocket of her red apron, pulling out a green envelope and hands it to me. She looks back and in a loud, booming voice shouts, "Do not open until Christmas!"

Chapter 11.

I hear the squeals of joy emanating from the living room, letting me know that Lake is up. As I emerge from the bathroom, he comes flying down the hallway

"Dad, Dad! Santa came early! I got a...a...blue...bike!" he says trying to catch his breath.

"What? Santa came already?" I place my hand over my heart as I pretend to be shocked and surprised. Lake grabs my hand tugging me into the living room.

"Did Santa come early because he knew about my transplant?" he asks as he sits on the floor ready to tear open his gifts. Kelly is on the couch all smiles and beautiful.

"It would seem so, my boy. Look at all these gifts." I sit down next to my son as Mom brings out steaming mugs of coffee and cocoa. Before I get my first sip, there is a knock on the door. Mom goes and answers it then she and Richard come back together.

"Papa! Look, Santa came early!" Lake jumps up and wraps his arms around his grandfather's waist.

"Well, what do you know; he sure did. Seems as though you were a very good boy this year. Look at all those gifts." After Lake releases him, Richard takes off his coat and sits at the end of the couch, close to where Lake is on the floor. We all gather around while Lake passes out gifts.

The last two presents left are for Mom and Kelly. My son hands the ladies their gifts. Mom tears hers open and is speechless. She has been admiring this watch for some time now—the one you can add your children's birthstones to on the face. I had Lake's and mine added. The waterworks begin as she holds the box, pulling the timepiece in to her heart. I hear Kelly gasp as she opens hers.

"Oh, Creek, it's beautiful. But I can't accept this. It's too much," she says, holding up the silver chain with a beautiful heart pendant. On the back, the words, *Lord, guide my hands and my heart as I care for my patients today,* are inscribed.

"Please accept it as a thank you for how wonderful you've been with my child this week." She looks at me, and her eyes are glossy, giving them an almost melted chocolate look.

"It was easy. Lake's an awesome kid. Thank you so much. This is nicest thing anyone has ever done for me." I stand to help her put on the necklace. She holds up her dark waves as I clasp it around her neck.

"Creek, this is for you." Richard hands me a small wrapped square box. I tear the paper off, opening the lid to find a set of keys. I looked at Richard puzzled.

"Go look in the driveway." He nods towards the window. I race over to the frosted glass, and there sits a brand new black SUV.

I hadn't noticed everyone followed behind me until Lake asks, "Is that ours?" I stare at the vehicle in awe and disbelief.

"Yes, grandson, it is. I figured this would be easier for you all, so Teri didn't have to catch rides to work when Lake has doctor appointments and such. It's tagged and insured for the next year." I turn and hug my ex-father-in-law. "Creek, she was a fool to walk away from such a good man. You never talk bad about her or to her. You don't keep her from seeing Lake. And if you had, it would be entirely understandable. You are a fabulous father who gave up everything you wanted to do to take care of your son. I just figured it was time you got something back in return." He squeezes me harder, and I can hear the sobs of the women behind me.

"Please, Richard, stay and spend the day with us?" He says yes.

Mom throws us out of the kitchen, so she can get started cooking supper. Richard grabs the coffee carafe and a mug as we sit back down in the living room and watch Lake play with his new toys.

Mom made a feast of turkey, dressing, mashed potatoes, gravy, homemade cranberry sauce, and a veritable array of pies and cakes. We use the living room to eat because there isn't enough space for us all in the kitchen. So, ladies lay- all the food out on the kitchen table, buffet-style, and we help ourselves, then grab a seat in the other room. Afterwards, we relax and conversate as Lake goes back to playing with his toys.

I begin clearing the dishes off the coffee table, and Kelly washes. I put the left-over food away and dry the dishes. We grab the fresh pot of coffee that we brewed and head back to join the others.

I forgot to get my boy some juice, so we stop for me to hand the carafe over to Kelly when Lake yells out, "Look up!" We do and notice we're standing under the mistletoe. "Now you have to kiss her!" He giggles.

"Oh, son, I don't think so," I say turning to go back into the kitchen.

"No, Dad you, have to! It's a Christmas rule." He looks at us with disapproving eyes.

I look at Kelly, and she looks up at me. I just shrug and go for it. I kiss her right on her lips. We are standing here lip to lip with people watching, but neither of us brakes away. Mom clears her throat. I guess that was her way of saying that's enough. We step back from one another. Then I open my eyes that I hadn't even noticed were closed. I see that her eyes are open, and her face is that cute shade pink it turns when she is embarrassed or being shy. She smiles at me, and I feel a flutter. I have only felt this way with one other person, but this is different. I can't describe it any other way, but it feels like the butterflies are bigger and filling a much larger space. I know it's weird, and I don't quite understand it myself.

Chapter 12.

Sleep eluded me last night. Not only did the thoughts of my son's procedure keep me restless, but the feel of the softest lips still lingered in my brain. Thank goodness Mom is riding with me to the children's hospital to get Lake checked in. They provide free hotel-like rooms for family to spend their time when they are not with their loved one.

I sit up, throwing my legs over the side of the couch where I decided to sleep, hoping my restlessness was due to the recliner. I hear Lake talking to Kelly about what his transplant will be like. I could barely look her in the eyes after that sweet kiss. When I did glance at her, she would deflect her eyes away from me.

We'll see what today holds, I suppose. I push myself off the couch to see what the boy wants for breakfast.

We have some time to spare before leaving this morning given we decided to pack the vehicles last night. After Lake's apple pie breakfast and my shower, we are ready to make the two-hour journey. Richard called earlier to say he would be at the hospital tomorrow. No word from Cindy; I know she'll make it. I am hoping, anyway. Lake grabs his backpack as we head out the door. Kelly will meet us at the hospital later; she was going to go home to unpack her car.

An hour into the drive and the boy is sleeping, so Mom figures this is the best time to discuss my love life or lack thereof. "What was that kiss about yesterday? Afterwards, you all barely spoke two words to each other." I'm not sure how to describe it to her even if I want to.

"Mom, it was just a harmless kiss to appease Lake. Nothing more, nothing less." Hopefully, that answer satisfies her.

"Creek Hollis, that girl turned pink, and your eyes went from almond shaped to hearts. Don't tell me it was nothing. I tell you all the time, boy, I'm your mother, and I can read every emotion that crosses your face." Yes, Ms. Teri Hollis knows me too well.

"Mom, please. It was nothing. Now can we drop it?" I know she can hear in my voice that I am uncomfortable talking to her about it. She changes the subject, and I'm relieved.

A little while later, we get all checked in, and my boy is happy with the room they've put him in. It's the Dr. Seuss room. There are life-size wall stickers of The Cat in the Hat, The Lorax, even The Grinch, displayed over every wall in the room. His hospital gown has Fox in Socks on it.

Dr. Courtney and Dr. Stokes walk in to explain what the procedure will entail. "Lake will receive the marrow through his port, or central venous catheter. This is what we call engraftment, and he will have these sessions daily during the upcoming week. There is no reason for him to be anesthetized. The procedure itself is fairly straightforward, but the recovery time can be a challenge. Side effects during the infusion of the marrow can include pain, chills, fever, hives, a drop in blood pressure, and possibly chest pains.

"Now, the hardest part is going to be staying here for several weeks so we can keep an eye on him and make sure the cells are doing their thing. Also, we have him on medication to prevent graft-versus-host disease (GVHD). Sometimes, the transplanted new cells (the graft) may attempt to attack the patient's tissues (the host), even if the donor is a relative. Lake will be confined to this room, and any visitor must wear a gown, mask, and gloves to prevent germs and keep him healthy.

"He will have regular blood draws, vitals checked. Of course, Creek, you already have one of our parent suites that will be yours for as long as your son is here.

"We will monitor him through the night, and when the donor cells get here in the morning, we will begin. Do you have any questions for us?" Dr. Stokes asks before he does a listen to Lake's heart.

"No, I think you covered everything, but if I think of anything, I'll let you know. Thank you." Just then, Kelly walks into the room, and Lake smiles instantly. I have to admit; I do as well.

*****

After many hours of playing board games with Mom, Kelly, and me, Lake finally falls asleep. I keep checking my phone to see if I have any messages from Cindy, and there are none. I sent Mom back to the suite to get some rest, but I can't slow down. Walking out into the hallway, I see Kelly standing at the nurses' station. Realizing I hadn't eaten since breakfast, I that way to let them know I will stepping away to go to the cafeteria.

"Hey, Kelly, I'm going to go to the cafeteria; I will be right back. If he wakes up looking for me, can you call my cell phone or text me?" She looks at her watch then back at me.

"The cafeteria is closed, but there's a diner about two blocks down that's open twenty-four hours. Can I tag along? They have the best Greek salad there." I nod, and she grabs her coat.

The elevator ride down to the lobby is quiet except for the soft sound of classical music playing. Once outside, Kelly follows me to my vehicle. It's been sitting awhile, so we hover inside, giving the engine time to warm up.

"Creek, this doesn't have to be awkward, you know." I look at her, trying to see where she is going with this conversation. "You've barely spoken to me since the kiss. It was a harmless kiss," she says looking down at her gloved hands.

"A harmless kiss that made your face turn pink and my stomach flutter." *Oh no, why did I say that?* I look over at her and the shocked expression on her face.

"Your stomach fluttered, too?" she asks in a low, shy voice. We sit looking at each other for a brief moment before something comes over us and laughter erupts.

"Kelly, I find you beautiful, smart, and so kind-hearted. Maybe these feelings stem from seeing you with Lake, and as you've noticed, his mom isn't around much."

"Or maybe, you like me," she says leaning over her seat to kiss my cheek.

"Or maybe, I like you. We've only known each other a week," I respond, holding her face in between my hands.

"They say all it can take is a glance." She is right. The first moment I met her in that room, I felt something—a pull.

We continue to stare into each other's eyes for a few more moments before my stomach growls so loud that Kelly lets out a hearty laugh.

"I think my butterflies have turned into lions. Let's go eat." I let her face go and put the car in drive in order to satisfy the beast in my belly.

Chapter 13.

Lake's transplant has begun. This session will take about two to three hours. He's been watching the Christmas parade on the wall-mounted television. They had me, Mom, and Richard put on sterile hospital garb and masks to help keep him infection-free.

This morning, the hospital had a Santa making room rounds, talking to all the kids. Lake was over-joyed to see the jolly fellow.

Kelly and I had a good, guess you could say, first date at the diner last night. We talked and laughed until tears were streaming down our faces. She is here now, taking vitals and watching the parade with the others. I am observing them all interact. Mom and Richard are talking politics and retirement. My mother says that retirement is for old folks, and to hear her tell it, she's a spry chicken. My boy is just enjoying having his family with him. All except for Cindy.

I can see in Richard's face that he is disappointed with his daughter not being here, but he doesn't let his grandson see it. I need coffee. Kelly must recognize my need for caffeine as she waves me out into the hall.

"Let's go to the Starbucks down in the lobby. My treat," she says. I begin to remove the mask and hospital clothes that I had to put over my street clothes and toss them in the dirty laundry bin. But as we walk past the nurses' station, a blonde calls my name, holding an envelope out to me.

"Mr. Hollis, this was just dropped off for you," she comments as I walk over to get the envelope. I look at it front and back. It just says my name on the front, so I open it to see who it's from.

Dear Creek,

I'm sure by now you're upset with me for not showing up for Lake's transplant. I wholeheartedly understand. But I couldn't come today because I am recovering from a procedure myself. Creek, I was our son's donor. I wanted to stay anonymous. Daddy doesn't even know. I don't wish for Lake to look at me as some type of hero. You, Creek, are the only hero in this story, and that's how I want him to view you.

What I did was what any person with a caring heart should do. What you do is what I, as a mother, never could, and that was care for that beautiful boy. I gave him the gift of life, but you, you gave him the gift of love. I can never get back

those years I chose to stay away, all I can do is be there for the next ones. Please don't tell him I am the donor; I did nothing spectacular. Again, you are the rightful hero. I will be to visit him as soon as I can.

Cindy

I can feel the tears rolling down my cheeks. "She was his donor," I say softly as Kelly stands beside me.

"Who was?" she asks while wiping my tears away.

"His mom. She came back to be his donor. She doesn't want him to know." I look at Kelly and hand her the letter. She reads and begins to cry herself, then she grabs my face between her hands and places a soft kiss on my lips in front of all her colleagues.

"You, Creek Hollis, are truly The Gift of Love."

Lake

My transplant took, and I'm in remission. My mom came to see me in the hospital to tell me she was back in Glorieville for good. She said she missed me, and well, I missed her a lot, too.

Dad and Kelly are boyfriend and girlfriend now, and my dad smiles a lot more now. Kelly is so fun. She comes over to cook for the two of us. She makes good soup, too. Don't tell Grandma.

When we came home from the hospital, Dad forgot about the envelope that Ms. Mary had given him at the diner, and it said not to open 'til Christmas. He did finally open it, and surprise, there were papers for him to sign to become part owner of the Country Kitchen. He cried.

Ms. Mary came over and brought me a strawberry cream pie and told my dad there was no one more responsible than him, and it would be an honor to have him help her run the diner.

Since I am in remission and there were no long-lasting side effects to my transplant, I will go to an actual school in September with other kids. I'm excited about that. Well, I need to go get in the car; Dad, Kelly, Mom, Nana, Papa, and I are going to a leukemia walkathon. For every mile I walk, money gets donated to help find a cure for this childhood disease. I'm going to walk hundreds!

Thank you for reading A Gift of Love.

Thanks to my family, for supporting me and my dreams! I love you sooo much!

To my reader family, you guys are the ones that keep me going and always striving to do something new! I Love each and every one of you!

To my author peeps who have inspired me, I love you sooo much!

To my PA, Kelly, we will win this fight! I love you!

To my editor, KA Matthews, thanks for sticking with me over the last two years. Without your editing skills, I would be lost!

To Courtney & Johnna, you ladies are the best!

To my reader group gals, you ladies truly hold my heart in your hands. I hope you continue to stick with me!

About the author

This is my first clean read...

Born and raised in Michigan, right outside of Detroit. I have two adult daughters and a Chihuahua, who is needier than my girls ever were. I have loved to read and write fiction stories since I was in elementary school.

Where you can find me.

Facebook-https://www.facebook.com/pages/Author-LJ-SeXton/734537879993958?fref=nf

Goodreads
https://www.goodreads.com/user/show/41049159-l-j-sexton

Twitter- https://twitter.com/SeXtonbooks

Instagram-
https://www.instagram.com/authorljsexton/

Website: http://ljsexton.weebly.com/

Other works by J. Grandison written as LJ Sexton

These are not clean reads!

Fixing Souls Novella Series

Fractured

Broken

Pieced 2Gether

Fixed Souls

Forgiving Souls Duology

(Can be read in tandem with the Fixing Souls)

Beginning Souls

Returning Souls

Forever Souls (can be read as standalone)

Secret Souls

All the Souls books can be found in a boxset on all major platforms.

M/M story

Until It Wasn't

(Co-Authored with Amy Robyn)

COMING SOON

Jumper Unloved

Ladies' Nyght MC

Made in United States
North Haven, CT
22 November 2021